ETHICAL

DEBATES

Energy Resources

RICHARD SPILSBURY

WAYLAND

First published in 2009
by Wayland

Wayland
338 Euston Road
London NW1 3BH

Wayland Australia
Level 17/207 Kent Street
Sydney NSW 2000

Commissioning editor: Jennifer Sanderson
Designer: Rita Storey
Picture researcher: Kathy Lockley
illustrator: Ian Thompson
Proofreader: Susie Brooks

British Library Cataloguing in
Publication Data
British Library Cataloguing in
Publication Data
Spilsbury, Richard, 1963-
Energy resources. - (Ethical debates)
1. Energy consumption - Moral and
ethical aspects -
Juvenile literature
I. Title
178

ISBN: 978-0-7502-5658-2

Printed in China

Wayland is a division of
Hachette Children's Books,
an Hachette UK company.
www.hachette.co.uk

Picture Acknowledgements:
The author and publisher would like to thank the following agencies for allowing these pictures to be reproduced: Arco Images GmbH/Alamy: 30; Arctic-Images/Corbis: 42; Yann Arthus-Bertrand/Corbis: 29; Rob Bowden/ EASI-images: Titlepage, 9; Skye Brackpool/Rex Features: 27; Andrew Brown/Ecoscene: 5; Adrian Cooper/EASI-images: 24; Corbis: 13; Philip James Corwin/Corbis: COVER, 26; Andrew Davies/Still Pictures: 31; Uli Deck/epa/Corbis: 33; Digitalvision/Getty Images 15, 18, 34; Chris Fairclough/EASI-images: 6; Getty Images: 17, 38; John Giles/PA Wire/PA Photos: 19; Paul Glendell/Alamy: 41; John Gress/Corbis: 10; Imagestate Media Partners Limited – Impact Photos/Alamy: 32; Igor Kostin/Sygma/Corbis: 23; Will & Denis McIntyre/Corbis: 16; MedioImages/ Corbis: 22; Jeremy Nicholl/Alamy: 36; Pelamis Wave Power: 44; Photofusion Picture Library/ Alamy: 8; Hans Strand/Corbis: 14; vario images GmbH & Co KG/Alamy: 21; Jim West/Alamy: 40; Doug Wilson/Alamy: 37 Every attempt has been made to clear copyright. Should there be any inadvertent omission please apply to the publisher for rectification.

About the Consultant: Rob Bowden is an educational consultant who has taught at three UK universities. He has written and advised on many educational publications.

Note: The website addresses (URLs) included in this book were valid at the time of going to press. However, because of the nature of the Internet, it is possible that some addresses may have changed, or sites may have changed or closed down since publication. While the authors and publishers regret any inconvenience this may cause the readers, no responsibility for any such changes can be accepted by either the authors or the publishers.

contents

Real-life case study

This case study highlights some of the issues that surround the debate on energy resources.

case study

Growing fuel

In 2005, the US government decided to encourage farmers to grow maize (corn) to be converted into bioethanol. They did this partly as a response to rising world oil prices and high levels of vehicle pollution, and partly to supply the growing number of US bioethanol distilleries. That year alone, the US government gave out nearly US$9 billion (£4.5 billion) in tax cuts, grants and loans to farmers and bioethanol producers. This made the fuel cheap enough for farmers to grow and for consumers to buy. By 2008, there were around 180 bioethanol distilleries creating 11 billion gallons of fuel, and there are plans to triple production by 2017.

Bioethanol is a major biofuel. It is made by converting sugar or starch in crops into ethanol, a type of alcohol, by a process called distillation. The main crops used for bioethanol are maize and sugar cane. Normal car engines can run on regular fuel mixed with some bioethanol, often called gasohol. Cars with specially fitted engines can use higher proportions of biofuels.

Supporters of biofuels say that burning bioethanol releases less energy but it also pollutes the atmosphere less than petrol or diesel. They also argue that by growing biofuels, the reliance on oil, a non-renewable resource, is greatly reduced.

Critics of the US biofuel expansion say that biofuels can do more harm than good. The United States' promotion of and demand for bioethanol absorbs 5 per cent of the world's cereal crops but has replaced less than 1 per cent of global oil use, so pollution from using oil has not been significantly reduced by biofuels. Creating bioethanol uses up oil and water, too. For example, oil is used to make fertilizers to help maize grow well and to power the pumps that are used to water fields. On average in the United States, the power in oil used to produce bioethanol is almost equal to the energy that bioethanol can produce in cars. Vast quantities of water are used to steam and heat maize during distillation in factories.

With more maize being grown in the United States, and more imported from other countries, the world price of maize for feeding people and their livestock rose. A World Bank senior economist concluded that the recent expansion in biofuels use has driven global food prices up by 75 per cent and this affects the poorest people. In Mexico, over 100 million people eat maize daily. However, US demand for maize has caused its price to double, triggering protests in January 2008, involving tens of thousands of people who could not afford to buy the food.

viewpoints

'It is clear that some biofuels have huge impacts on food prices. All we are doing by supporting these is subsidizing higher food prices, while doing nothing to tackle climate change.'

Dr David King, UK government's former chief scientific adviser, 2008.

'Corn ethanol is the most successful alternative fuel commercially available in the US today.'

Barack Obama, US President, 2007

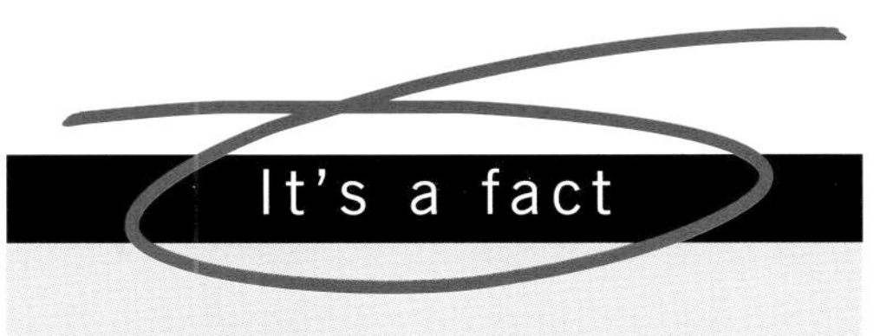

Gasohol called E10 contains 10 per cent ethanol mixed with gasoline, while E85 contains 85 per cent ethanol. Parts in engines that can run on E85 are made from materials such as stainless steel that are not damaged by acidic ethanol.

▼ Fuel farming is a growing industry in the maize-growing belt of the United States. This is a plant for turning maize to ethanol in Minnesota, United States.

CHAPTER 1

What are energy resources?

Energy resources include oil and moving water, which people use to produce heat, movement (kinetic) or electrical energy. Heat is used to cook and warm homes. Kinetic energy is used to run machines, from buses and diggers that help carry out work to generators that produce electricity. Appliances, such as computers, fridges and light bulbs, could not work without electricity or power.

Renewable and non-renewable

There are two types of energy resources, non-renewable and renewable. Non-renewable resources include coal, gas, oil and nuclear fuel. These are likely to run out as there is a limited supply of them on the planet. However, renewable resources, such as sunlight and ocean tides, are in endless supply and therefore should never run out.

Fossil fuels

Oil, coal and natural gas are all fossil fuels. These built up millions of years ago in the Earth's crust. The remains of ancient swamp forests and marine organisms were buried beneath many layers of mud that turned into rock. The trapped remains were gradually changed into carbon-rich fossil fuels by the high pressures and temperatures underground. Fossil fuels are

▼ This power station in Spain uses fossil fuels to generate electricity.

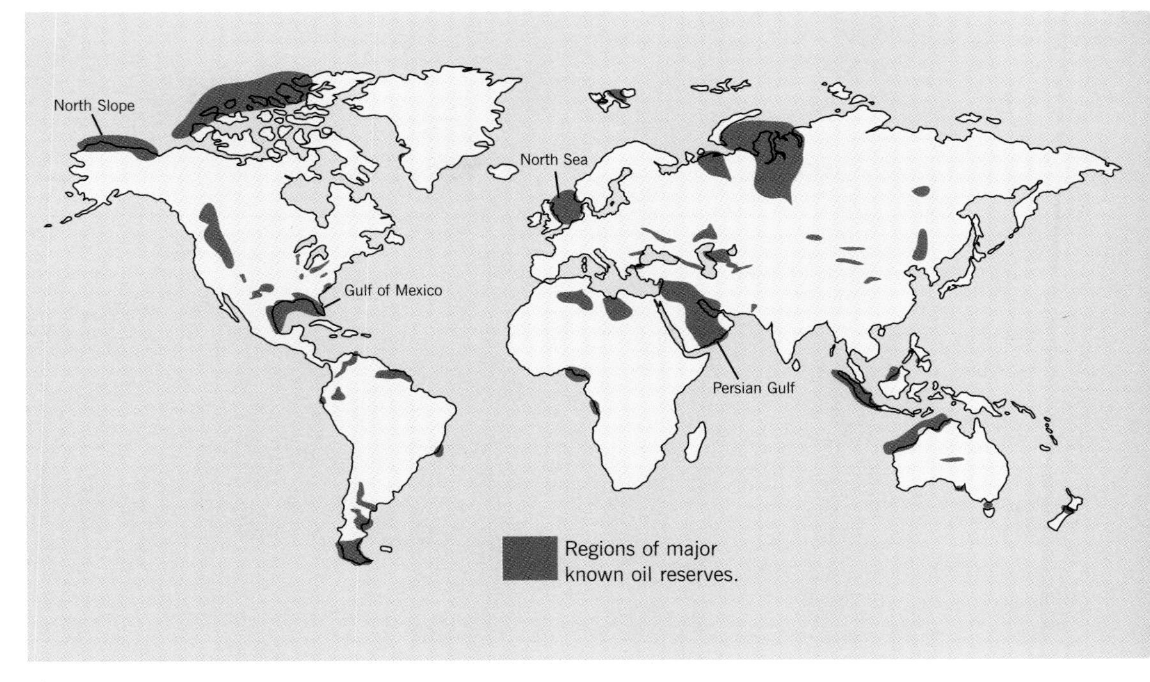

▲ The major oil reserves are located all around the world, but the greatest quantities of oil come from the Persian Gulf region.

non-renewable because they took so long to form and, more recently, such large areas of swamp forest and ocean have not been buried to take their place. Therefore, there is not a new supply to take the place of what people have used.

In some places coal and oil are exposed at the surface and are easily dug up, but most fossil fuels are mined or drilled from where they are trapped, deep under the surface. Fossil fuels are heated until they react with oxygen in air, or burn, to release large amounts of heat energy. Most of the coal used worldwide is burned in power stations to create steam. The steam is pressurized, and the force of the steam hitting turbine blades spins them around. This turns generators, which are machines that convert the spinning movement into power. Some oil and gas is also used as fuel in power stations, but most is converted into petrol or diesel fuels to run the engines in vehicles and other machines.

It's a fact

There are three types of coal. Lignite is soft and dark brown and contains 70 per cent carbon. Bituminous coal is darker and harder, with 85 per cent carbon. Anthracite is black, shiny and hard, with up to 98 per cent carbon. When anthracite burns, it releases more heat per gram and less polluting smoke into the atmosphere than the other types. However, as anthracite deposits are rare globally, most of the coal used is lignite and bituminous that release less energy and create more pollution.

Nuclear fuel

Worldwide, just over 6 per cent of all power is created using energy from another non-renewable energy resource – nuclear fuel. The most common nuclear fuel is uranium, a metal found in rocks. There are different kinds of uranium, but the type used as an energy resource is uranium-235 (U-235). This is made up of atoms that can split open easily when they are bombarded with particles called neutrons, releasing vast amounts of heat, radiation and more neutrons. These neutrons split open further U-235 atoms and so on, creating a chain reaction that releases dangerously large amounts of energy when it is not controlled.

▲ Turbines under the Rance tidal power plant have operated using the rise and fall of water in the Rance river estuary in Brittany, France, since 1967

However, in nuclear power plants, the speed of reaction is controlled. Several long metal fuel rods containing U-235 are at the heart of the reactor that creates heat. Control rods made from a substance called boron can be lowered amongst the fuel rods to slow the reaction. They do this by absorbing neutrons and therefore stopping more atoms from splitting. Water or gas in the reactor absorbs and carries away heat to be used to make steam, just as in a coal-fired power station.

Renewable resources

Around the world, renewable energy resources – water, the tides, wind, sunlight and biomass – supply about the same amount of energy put together as nuclear fuel. Hydropower is created when water flowing down a river or from a reservoir through a dam turns turbines to generate power. Tidal power uses the daily tides of water in estuaries to generate power in a similar way. Wind turbines, usually raised high in the air where wind is stronger, rotate and generate power using the moving air. Winds acting on the surface of oceans produce waves, whose energy can also be harvested using turbines.

Energy from the Sun, Earth's nearest star, is harnessed to produce power directly using solar or photovoltaic (PV) cells.

These generate currents of electricity between sandwiched layers of silicon, set between glass or plastic layers. Other solar systems used to create power include trough-shaped mirrors that focus the Sun's heat onto oil-filled tubes. The hot oil then heats water to create steam for turbines. Solar collectors are panels that warm water in tubes to heat houses. The other source of heat used to make power is geothermal energy, which comes from hot rocks deep underground.

Biomass energy comes from plant or animal matter. This can be burnt directly or allowed to rot to produce a gas for burning. It ranges from wood and manure to gases produced from landfill sites. Most biomass is grown on plantations or farms to ensure a large and constant supply of fuel. Biomass crops include quick-growing trees such as eucalyptus, willow and oil palms. Critics of biomass energy argue that these resources are only renewable when people plant crops to replace all those they harvest.

It's a fact

Scientists estimate that solar energy offers about 100 times the potential of global wind energy, and around 2,000 times that of geothermal energy. The amount of energy people around the world use each year is equivalent to one-six-thousandth of the solar energy that reaches the Earth.

viewpoints

'The use of solar energy has not been opened up because the oil industry does not own the Sun.'
Ralph Nader, US independent presidential candidate, 2008

'...fossil fuels... are likely to retain a significant role in the global energy system through this century and far beyond, and the transition toward renewables and perhaps nuclear will be gradual.'
Professor Mark Jaccard, *Sustainable Fossil Fuels*, 2005

▼ Oilseed rape is just one of the crops that can be harvested to produce biofuels.

Choosing resources

Different countries produce power from various mixes of energy resources. This mix depends on a variety of factors. One is location. In Norway and Canada, over 90 per cent of power is hydropower because these countries have plentiful mountains and rivers to fill reservoirs. The greatest wave and wind energy is produced in locations between latitudes of 40 degrees and 60 degrees, such as Scotland or southern Africa, where the cold polar air meets warm tropical air and creates regular winds. Another factor affecting the energy mix is the availability of natural resources. China's power stations burn mostly lignite as this is the only type of coal found in the country, and is therefore cheaper than better quality coal that would have to be transported from elsewhere.

Choice of resources is also a consequence of wealth or political will. In poorer countries such as Nepal, Vietnam or Mali, power from a centralized grid is available only to small sections of the population. Most communities in such countries can afford to use only biomass or small-scale hydropower installations. In some countries, governments promote particular energy resources. For example, the German government collects an energy tax from its citizens to help subsidize the spread of solar power, making Germany a leader in solar technology. France, however, produces 80 per cent of its power using nuclear energy. The reasons for this include a long history of nuclear research in the country and the desire to be independent of oil-producing countries. In the 1970s, France relied on oil for fuel in

▼ Increasing global air travel is putting pressure on fossil fuel resources. An average passenger aircraft uses around 10 litres of fuel to travel 1 kilometre.

It's a fact

In 2007, there were over 76 million flights globally.

its power stations, but a global problem in oil supply and high costs meant it quickly developed nuclear power plants to supply its electricity.

Increasing energy use

In recent years, issues concerning which energy resources to choose have become a matter of great debate around the world. This is partly due to the fact that people today are using far more energy than they did in the past. During the twentieth and twenty-first centuries, electrical appliances have become commonplace in wealthier countries. This has often followed the expansion of power stations burning fossil fuels and networks of long-distance cables to distribute the electricity that they generate into homes, businesses and other user destinations.

Increasing energy use is also the result of a growing global population, and the increasing globalization of trade, where products made in, say, China are sold around the world. Even though today's electrical appliances, vehicles and power stations can use energy far more efficiently than those in the past, manufacturers continue to make power-hungry machines that people continue to buy as they are cheaper. Using any energy resource has environmental, social and economic consequences, so the pros and cons have to be considered carefully.

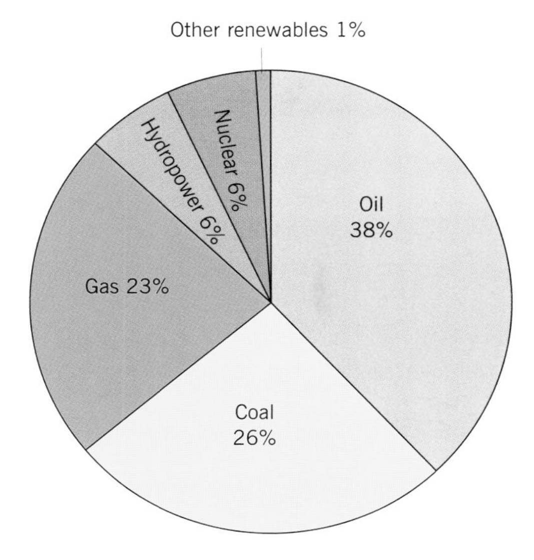

▲ Fossil fuels provided around 87 per cent of the energy used in 2008. Nuclear and hydropower supplied most of the rest.

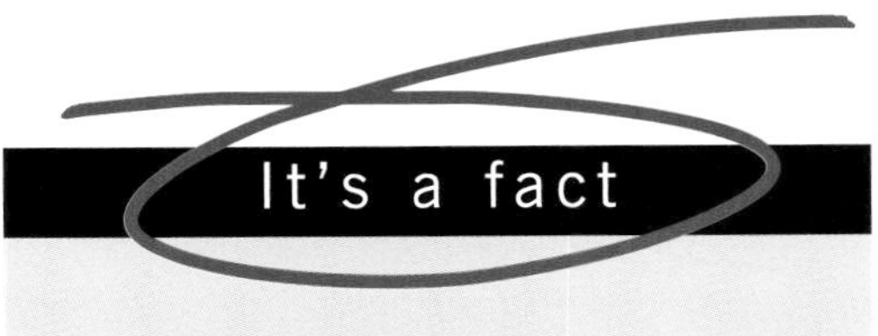

The United States has 5 per cent of the world's population but uses 25 per cent of global energy.

summary

- Energy resources can be non-renewable, such as coal and oil, or renewable, such as wind or solar.
- Power is made by converting movement energy, usually via heating water to make steam, into electrical energy.
- The types of energy resources available to countries depend on factors including geography and wealth.
- Many energy resources are under increasing pressure, owing to higher demand from an increasing population.

CHAPTER 2

Fuels from the past

Fossil fuels are at the heart of the energy debate. The major problem is that burning these fuels to release heat energy also releases gases that cause changes in the atmosphere. These gases are contributing to global climate change as a result of the greenhouse effect and are also causing harmful air pollution. There are problems with extracting and transporting fossil fuels, too.

Greenhouse effect

In a greenhouse, energy from the Sun shines through the glass that then traps heat inside, helping plants to grow and fruits and vegetables to ripen faster. A similar effect occurs in the atmosphere around the Earth. Our planet gets nearly all of its heat energy from the Sun. Solar energy travelling through the atmosphere is absorbed by the Earth's surface, which then radiates heat back towards space.

Certain gases in the atmosphere, including carbon dioxide, methane and water vapour, absorb some of the Sun's heat energy. These are called greenhouse gases as they trap heat much like the glass in a greenhouse. Without this natural greenhouse effect, most of the Sun's heat would disappear into space and the average surface temperature around the world would be 30 degrees Centigrade cooler. This would be too cold, not only for people but also for the majority of other organisms to survive.

Changing the balance

Up until the nineteenth century, the proportion of carbon dioxide in the atmosphere remained fairly constant. Scientists know this from analyzing bubbles of air trapped in deep ice at Antarctica and from other clues around the globe. Many organisms, from people to bacteria, produce carbon dioxide during respiration. Green plants and some ocean planktons take in carbon dioxide and convert it into food, using energy from sunlight, in a process called photosynthesis. Some carbon dioxide dissolves in the oceans, weathers rocks or is used by ocean animals to make shells and there is a natural balance between carbon dioxide production and absorption.

However, this balance of carbon dioxide has been upset by people burning fossil fuels. The ancient carbon trapped in the fuels reacts with oxygen, producing carbon dioxide in addition to energy. Since 1750, the concentration of carbon dioxide in the atmosphere has increased by more than 30 per cent. This rise in proportion has created a stronger greenhouse effect. The current global average temperature of around 14 degrees Centigrade is around 1 degree Centigrade warmer than it was in 1750.

It's a fact

Oil and gas are running out faster than coal, so they are becoming more expensive and less widely available. More countries are building new coal-fired power plants or starting to use coal in plants that formerly used other fossil fuels. However, burning coal produces more greenhouse gases than burning gas and oil.

In some parts of Earth, the temperature rise has been enough to melt glaciers and ice caps that previously remained frozen for millennia. While rising temperatures are increasing greenhouse gas proportions in the atmosphere, researchers at Bristol University in the United Kingdom (UK) have discovered that plants on land are also absorbing less carbon as the air gets warmer. Warm seawater dissolves less carbon dioxide than colder water and warmer air temperatures evaporate more water vapour into the atmosphere. As frozen land thaws, soil bacteria rot more plant and animal waste, releasing methane. The combination of less carbon dioxide being absorbed and increased water vapour and methane in the atmosphere is making matters worse by further enhancing the greenhouse effect.

▼ The light blue shape below is a dense group of millions of plankton off the Atlantic coast. Photosynthesis by ocean plankton removes about 100 million tonnes of carbon dioxide from the atmosphere each day overall. Rising ocean temperatures are reducing this capacity for carbon.

Temperature and climate effects

The impact of the greater greenhouse effect is expected to increase further over the coming decades. This is because carbon dioxide remains in the atmosphere for approximately 200 years, so carbon dioxide added today simply adds to that produced in the past. Global temperatures are expected to rise by up to 4–6 degrees Centigrade during the next century. This will be enough to melt ice at the North Pole all year around. The meltwater (water released from melting ice), and the fact that warmer ocean water takes up more space than cold water, could increase global sea levels by about 50 centimetres by 2100. Currently, around the world, there are 100 million people in coastal communities that would be inundated by this sea level rise. The warmth is also expected to increase the spread of diseases carried by insects, such as mosquitoes, that can breed only in warm, moist conditions.

Increased heat is already changing world weather. Weather is driven by contrasts in temperature and humidity of air and also the temperature of water masses across the planet. Rising temperatures are therefore creating stronger storms, longer droughts, and worse flooding following heavy rainfall in different parts of the world.

Who is responsible for climate change?

Most scientists agree that the only way to slow climate change is to produce fewer greenhouse gases. At a 1997 meeting of the United Nations in Kyoto, Japan, many countries agreed the maximum carbon dioxide they could emit through power generation and transport, in order to slow climate change in future. This agreement, called the Kyoto Protocol raised several debates.

The United States refused to sign the Protocol because the fast-developing countries of China and India were not required to reduce their emissions. In 2006, China's emissions topped the world lists at 6,200 million tonnes of carbon dioxide and new fossil fuel power stations

The frozen Arctic Ocean is the hunting ground of polar bears. Global warming will shrink their habitat considerably.

A traffic jam creates fumes on the M25 orbital motorway around London, UK. All car users worldwide contribute to the problem of increasing greenhouse emissions.

were being built at a rate of two per week. The United States believes that as China is the worst greenhouse culprit, it should be made to cut emissions, too.

Is the developed world right to put the blame for climate change on developing countries? China is the fastest-growing emitter of carbon dioxide because of a massive expansion in fossil fuel power stations, which supply growing industry and domestic demand in the country. However, this is mirroring the ways that richer nations developed in the past. Scientists estimate that since 1850, the United States has emitted 30 per cent of all greenhouse gases ever produced by people. What is more, many people argue that much of the Chinese power and labour is being used to make cheap products that will be sold by richer nations, such as the UK and the United States, for profit. Many people believe that population size should also be considered. For example, the emissions per person in China are less than one-quarter of those in the United States.

▲ Acid rain damaged this forest on Mt Mitchell in western North Carolina, United States.

Air pollution

Another major debate around fossil fuels is how much pollution they cause. Burning coal and diesel fuel releases gases, including sulphur dioxide and nitrous oxides, into the atmosphere. It also releases fine particles of soot resulting from carbon in the fuels not burning properly. Gas and particulate air pollution have many effects. One of the most detrimental effects of particulate air pollution is that the gases mix with water vapour in the atmosphere to produce acid rain.

Not only can acid rain can gradually dissolve the soft rock used in buildings, but it also has damaging effects on natural habitats. It can kill sensitive organisms, such as frogs and fish in lakes and bacteria in soils. It also causes nutrient loss and damage in leaves and buds, so plants such as trees become unhealthy and even die.

Particulate pollution can affect people's health, too. The fine particles can cause noses and eyes to run and also irritate the sensitive tissues in throats and lungs, causing breathing problems, which may also trigger serious asthma attacks or heart problems. In addition, particulates and gases can combine with ozone gas, dust and sunlight creating brown smog clouds. Smog concentrates and traps air pollution, especially over cities such as Los Angeles in the United States and Mexico City, Mexico, which are surrounded by high mountains that prevent winds from blowing the air away.

case study

Olympic air

Beijing, China has sometimes been called 'Greyjing', owing to the polluted air that sits over the city. The air pollution is a greyish mixture of emissions from factories, power stations, vehicle exhausts and dust that regularly blows off the Gobi desert, north of Beijing. Scientists have long known of the dangers of Beijing air to its residents. A 2002 study by Beijing University linked 25,000 premature deaths with airborne particles in polluted air. In 2005, the European Space Agency found that Beijing and neighbouring provinces had the planet's worst levels of nitrogen dioxide, which can cause fatal damage to people and other animals' lungs.

The Chinese government took decisive action to clean up 'Greyjing' during the ten years before it hosted the 2008 Olympic Games. They wanted the Games to be a showcase for their country and did not want visitors and athletes to stay away or avoid events owing to air pollution.

When pollution limits lung function and potentially triggers asthma attacks and coughing, it affects athletes' potential to win medals, especially in endurance events such as the marathon. The government spent US$20 billion (£10 billion) on doubling the number of subway lines, building vast areas of urban parks, and fitting factories with clean-air technology that removed more pollutants. The city also replaced 50,000 taxis and 10,000 buses with environment-friendly vehicles.

In the months leading up to the Games, particulate levels in city air had reduced, but they were still over 100 milligrams per cubic metre, around twice the safe level. So city officials ordered half of the city's 3.3 million vehicles off the roads, halted building work and temporarily closed many factories. The air for the Olympic athletes and tourists was cleaner than it had been for a decade, and the Games were a great success, but what will happen to 'Greyjing' in the future?

◀ Two days before the opening ceremony of the Beijing Olympics, the Bird's Nest Stadium was covered in a layer of smog.

Extracting fossil fuels

Mining coal can have enormous effects on ecosystems and communities. The obvious effects are large scars in the landscape, which are left by giant open-cast coal mines. When rainwater washes through piles of waste rock removed to access coal, it forms acids that dissolve poisonous metals. This acid mine drainage can pollute groundwater supplies. Piles of mine waste may collapse and choke rivers, causing flooding, or create landslides that threaten transport routes and communities. However, those who support the use of coal as an energy source say that polluting mine drainage and problems caused by mine waste are an issue for all types of mining, not just coal mining.

Coal mining releases large amounts of methane, a greenhouse gas, into the atmosphere, adding to the problem of global warming. Surface fires in coal-mining areas can set alight unmined coal underground. These fires are incredibly difficult to extinguish and can persist for decades or even centuries. The town of Centralia in Pennsylvania, United States, is now deserted owing to an underground fire accidentally started in 1962. The fire burned so much coal and made the ground so hot that it collapsed and it became unsafe to live in the town. Global coal fires release as much carbon dioxide each year as the total emissions from cars and other road vehicles.

Oil pollution

Oil can cause serious damage to ecosystems around the world. Spills from wells and supertankers or pipelines that transport the oil, create floating slicks on the world's oceans. Oil can also coat and kill animal and plant colonies, such as coral reefs and mangrove swamps, which are home to a rich variety of wildlife. Animals such as seabirds eat oil when they try to clean it off their feathers and as a result are poisoned. Oil also destroys the waterproofing of feathers, so birds get cold in seawater and can die. The drilling fluids that people pump down oil wells to release oil from rocks can also pollute marine environments and freshwater supplies.

Gas problems

Disturbances to the Earth caused by fossil fuel drilling can create major problems. For example, an Indonesian company drilling for gas in East Java in 2006 released trapped underground water that turned soft surface soil into mud. The mud has erupted continuously since then and has buried several villages, displacing around 30,000 people.

◀ This is just one of hundreds of oiled seabirds following the *Sea Empress* oil spill off western Wales, UK, in 1996.

▲ In 2008, UK protestors against coal-fired power stations publicized their 'Leave it in the Ground' campaign by stopping a coal train.

case study

Carbon protests

Many people feel that the greatest problems facing the planet are climate change and global warming, and that governments and private companies are being too slow to make changes. In 2005, the Campaign for Climate Change organized protests in 32 countries against the United States' failure to sign the Kyoto Protocol (see page 14). Power plants and new airports or road projects are often the focus for protests about emissions. In 2008, protestors boarded and prevented coal trains from moving their cargo to power plants in both Australia and the UK. The protestors felt that the publicity they attracted raised awareness about making energy choices to combat rising emissions. They insisted that stopping a coal delivery and drawing attention to the direct action would make the plant owners improve plant efficiency.

summary

- Extracting fossil fuels can damage and pollute land and ocean habitats.
- Burning fossil fuels increases greenhouse gases, such as carbon dioxide, in the atmosphere and contributes to climate change.
- Burning fossil fuels causes air pollution, which leads to problems such as acid rain.

CHAPTER 3

The nuclear option

Some people believe that nuclear power is the best solution to world power demand. Only small amounts of nuclear fuel are needed to release vast amounts of energy and there are virtually no greenhouse emissions from a nuclear reactor. However, nuclear energy is controversial. Not only does it create dangerous waste that needs special storage, but accidents at nuclear power plants are also potentially catastrophic.

Cheapest power?

Those who are in favour of nuclear power use price as one of their main arguments. In 2003, a unit of nuclear power cost 60 per cent more than a unit of power generated using fossil fuels. This unit price takes into account the cost of creating nuclear fuel and also removing old, contaminated nuclear power plants. This can cost up to US$6 billion (£3 billion) each. However, in recent years, world fossil fuel prices have doubled, so nuclear power may be cheaper than other types of power. Supporters of nuclear power say that it is definitely much cheaper when the true cost of emissions is considered. In the future, the cost of climate change may include failed harvests owing to changing weather, the cost of clearing up after hurricanes and floods, and the costs of flood defences defending coastal communities from rising sea levels. The spiralling cost of fossil fuels and Kyoto demands (see page 14) to generate fewer emissions are the major reasons why the UK, for example, made plans in 2006 to build many more nuclear power plants.

Radioactive waste

Once the uranium in fuel rods has been used to release heat, it becomes spent fuel, containing newly created radioactive substances, including plutonium and the gas krypton. This radioactive waste releases gamma radiation. Gamma radiation is extremely hazardous and can pass through materials such as steel. It can also change normal body cells into cancerous ones. The spent fuel is cooled in ponds for several months, then about 40 per cent of it is recycled or reprocessed into new fuel. The remaining 60 per cent is treated as waste that needs to be stored.

Nuclear waste is sealed in glass, then in concrete-filled barrels. Finally, it is buried in reinforced concrete bunkers. Initially it is referred to as high-level waste as it emits massive amounts of radiation for decades. High-level waste makes up just 1 per cent of the volume of all nuclear waste. Gradually, the waste becomes less harmful. Intermediate-level waste includes the water used to cool spent fuel rods and the waste created during reprocessing. Low-level waste is the least harmful as it releases very little radiation over thousands of years. It includes the tools used to mine uranium and workers' clothing, which is contaminated with radioactive dust or particles. The low-level waste may just be sealed in steel drums and stored in special dumps.

Storage in the future

One of the big nuclear debates is about long-term waste storage. By 2020, around

445,000 tonnes of spent fuel will have been generated. There are not enough safe places on Earth's surface to store the waste, so there are plans to bury it deep in old mines. For example, the US government plans to develop a deep storage site beneath Yucca Mountain, Nevada, as a national nuclear waste repository. Opponents of nuclear energy say that plans to store this waste underground are flawed. Earth movements in future could damage storage vessels and release radiation. Groundwater could also become contaminated with radioactive particles. Supporters of nuclear power say that the waste has been safely stored since the 1950s, when nuclear power plants were first developed. They say that going underground is safe and that high-level waste becomes easier to store with time so it is not a problem.

viewpoints

'It is a colossal mistake to head off down the nuclear path once again. We need a solution to climate change that protects the environment rather than threatens it, and one that does not literally cost the Earth.'

Ken Livingstone, former London Mayor, UK

'It's hard to see how we're going to get enough energy with low carbon emissions without nuclear playing a significant role.'

Professor Jeffrey Sachs, Director of the Earth Institute at Columbia University, United States

▼ These workers are in the high-tech control facility at a nuclear power station in Germany.

Zero emissions?

Nuclear power plants produce neither air pollution nor carbon dioxide during the nuclear reaction, unlike the burning reaction in fossil fuel powered machines. However, the mining of uranium, the conversion of uranium to fuel and the reprocessing of spent fuel all use power, and in doing so, create emissions. This energy use is set to increase in the future as companies have to mine deeper to find good uranium sources. In addition, it takes energy to build new nuclear power plants and take apart old ones, just as it does conventional power plants. Supporters of nuclear power say that even though nuclear is not a zero-emission energy source, it produces fewer emissions than fossil fuels; a nuclear power plant would use 74 kilograms of fuel in a year to produce 1,250 megawatts of power and would be responsible for around 400,000 tonnes of carbon dioxide emissions. In contrast, to generate the same power using fossil fuels, 8,600 tonnes of coal would need to be burned, releasing 22 times more carbon dioxide.

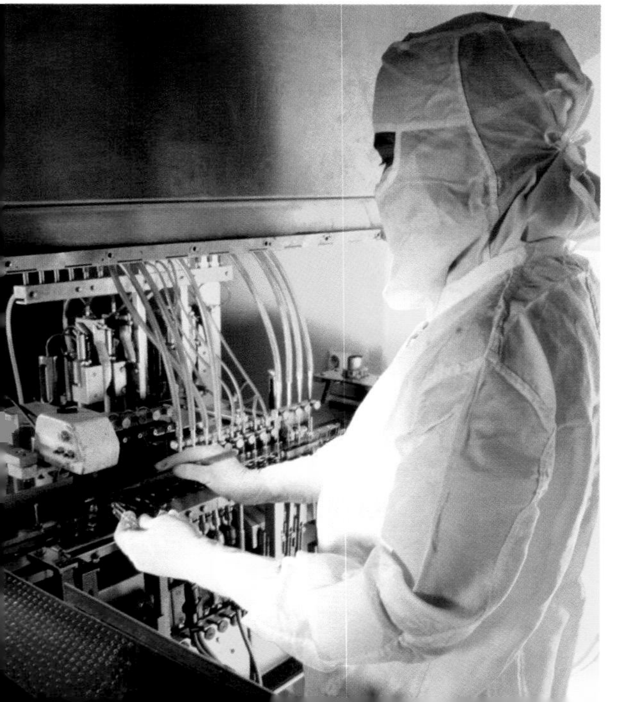

Nuclear accidents

Nuclear power stations are not atomic bombs waiting to go off, and are unlikely to melt down during accidents. The nuclear reaction is slowed by the presence of U-238 in fuel rods, a form of uranium that slowly releases neutrons. If the reactor becomes too hot, emergency control rods automatically drop into the reactor to shut it down. Pressure chambers around the reactor also have inbuilt cooling systems to prevent the reactor from becoming too hot. Many automatically flood the reactor with water or nitrogen to absorb neutrons and close down the reaction.

There have been serious accidents at nuclear power plants. The worst happened at Chernobyl in the Ukraine in 1986. Supporters of nuclear power say that the accident is testament to human error and that today's safety systems are even more advanced than in the 1980s. But critics point out that people do make errors and machinery can go wrong.

Fuel to weapons

Critics are also concerned about nuclear fuels being used to make atomic bombs. When uranium is refined and U-238 removed, the proportion of U-235 increases. The fuel is said to be enriched as it is more reactive. If this process is continued, the enriched fuel turns into unstable bomb material. Many countries, including Iran and North Korea, have enrichment technology. Governments of other countries ask whether this is to make fuel or bombs. Do countries such as the United States and the UK, both with enrichment technology themselves, have the right to say that Iran or North Korea cannot access this form of energy production?

◀ This female worker at a nuclear power plant is wearing protective clothing and a face mask.

▲ The thick concrete and steel structure of the Chernobyl reactor was destroyed by the blaze in 1986. Engineers wearing protective gear cleared radioactive debris from all around into the reactor and then encased the whole structure in concrete to contain the radioactivity.

case study

Chernobyl fallout

In 1986 at the Chernobyl nuclear power plant in the Ukraine, engineers overrode the safety system during a test. The nuclear reaction was then uncontrolled and released too much energy, blowing out the containment system. The resultant heat caused a giant fire. This released a huge cloud of fallout (radioactive dust) into the atmosphere.

Winds blew the fallout across Europe, contaminating more than 200,000 square kilometres of land. Scientists predicted that thousands of people would die in the months, years and decades after the accident, but in fact only 60 people died. These people were the emergency workers who were exposed to high levels of radiation immediately after the explosion. Thousands of people developed cancers, though many of these were treatable.

summary

- Nuclear power produces large amounts of power at a reasonable price, with minimal emissions.
- Nuclear power is controversial because the waste is radioactive and highly dangerous. Nuclear accidents are potentially catastrophic, and spent fuel can be used to create atomic bombs.
- In the long term, safety in storing nuclear waste is a highly contentious issue.

CHAPTER 4

Renewable energy

Renewable energy resources may seem to be the obvious answer to problems caused by non-renewables. Renewable energy sources produce low or zero emissions, minimal pollution and waste problems, and they are not running out. However, the benefits of renewables need to be balanced against their environmental, social and economic costs.

It's a fact

According to the energy corporation, BP, global investment in the construction of renewable energy production facilities was around US$71 billion (£35.5 billion) in 2007. Of this, Germany spent approximately 20 per cent.

Predictability of power

People need predictable power to meet their needs. Fossil fuel and nuclear power stations can keep working constantly, as long as there is enough fuel and they can match the output with demand from consumers – for example, there is greater demand for electricity during working hours than at night. However, renewable energy resources vary through time. The Sun shines only during the day, so solar power is not available at night, unless it is stored as electricity in batteries or as heat in other materials. Storage systems gradually lose power, making generation less efficient. Although wind blows at

▼ The solar panels in this building in Los Angeles, United States, have been designed as an architectural feature of the building.

different speeds during the day and night, it is generally abundant in winters when people need power to heat buildings. Geothermal power and hydropower can offer power at any time of year. The Earth constantly creates internal heat but it is economical to pump water underground to access this resource only in locations where the Earth's crust is thin, such as in parts of New Zealand. Some hydropower systems have a reservoir on either side of a dam. After water from the upper reservoir has passed through the turbines in the dam to the lower reservoir, electric pumps carry water back into the upper reservoir. The same water is then used to generate more power. In other hydropower systems, output varies by season as rivers flow into the upper reservoir varies.

Different scales

One advantage of renewable energy sources, such as solar or wind power, is that they can be accessed by individuals or communities on a small scale. People can connect up PV cells, a small wind turbine or an array of these devices to generate their own power. In some poorer countries, or parts of richer countries without access to central electricity grids, off-grid renewables are the only option. Microgeneration systems supply power at a higher unit of electricity cost than large-scale power plants on grids fed by many power plants. However, they are cheaper to set up and have a lower environmental cost as they do not need wide-ranging distribution systems for their electricity.

Price of power

One reason why some people support nuclear- or coal-generated power is that they are cheaper than renewable power. Solar power is by far the most expensive and costs about US$0.26 (13 pence) to produce 1 kilowatt of power per hour, while it costs just US$0.02 (one penny) to produce the equivalent nuclear power and just US$.03 (just over one penny) for the equivalent gas power. However, is it fair to make this comparison without taking into account the costs of climate change resulting from emissions, as well as pollution and social and economic disruption?

Biomass and hydropower are the two renewables currently cheap enough to compete with fossil fuel and nuclear power. One reason is that they have been heavily subsidized by governments to make them competitive. Surely it would be fair to the the solar and wind power industries to subsidize them, too? This is happening in some parts of the world. In Germany, the government buys back any spare power generated from renewables at a fair and guaranteed price. This encourages more people to set up renewable systems.

viewpoints

'While it is unlikely to impact energy bills before 2010, in 2020 both gas and electricity bills will be higher due to the cost of renewable energy, and it is important to recognize that.'
Malcolm Wicks, UK Energy Minister, 2007

'I challenge our nation to commit to producing 100 per cent of our electricity from renewable energy and truly clean carbon-free sources within 10 years.'
Al Gore, Nobel prize-winning climate change crusader, 2008

Wind farms, such as this one in Spain, need to have many turbines on one site to generate sufficient power at a competitive price for consumers.

Wind issues

Wind energy resources are most usually harvested using groups or farms of tall wind turbines. Turbines usually consist of three blades on a hub that turn on a tower tens of metres tall, because wind is stronger high above the ground. A 1-kilometre square wind farm containing 15 turbines, each generating 1 megawatt hour, can produce enough power for a town of 2,000 people in a more economically developed country. The same area could supply even more people in a less developed country where each household uses less power.

The fact that wind farms can be seen from kilometres away is one of the main issues regarding wind power. Some people say that wind farms spoil the look of the upland environments where they are often built. They also say that they may make homes near to turbines difficult to sell. Critics of wind farms also claim that the fast-moving turbine blades create a distracting thumping noise and shadow effects for people who live nearby. The blades can injure or kill passing birds, too. Critics argue that wind farms are inefficient at generating electricity and the emissions created during their manufacture outweigh their output. Supporters of wind farms say that the turbines' appearance is acceptable because they do not produce emissions as they work. They that say the noise is comparable to cars passing on a road, a noise that many people are so used to that they do not even notice it.

Off shore wind farms

Many major wind farm developments in richer countries are happening offshore, far away from people. It is more costly to install turbines in foundations under the sea, but the space is cheaper and more easily available than upland areas in many populous, richer countries such as the UK. Winds fluctuate less at sea than on land and have no obstructions, from buildings to hills, to affect their flow. This is very important as varying wind energy makes most onshore turbines operate at less than half of their generating capacity.

Solar power

Energy from the Sun is completely free and abundant, but creating solar power is not so simple or cheap. Pure silicon, used in the most common PV panels, is rare and it is an expensive, power-hungry process to purify silicon from its two main sources, sand and quartz crystal. Silicon cells are not particularly efficient either. They can convert less than 20 per cent of the energy in sunlight into power. Combining silicon with other substances, such as germanium, can increase the power, but refining these substances often causes pollution. Cheaper, plastic PV cells are being developed but these have a short life, so are likely to contribute to global waste problems.

Solar arrays (collections of PV cells) take up large amounts of space. For example, the Juwi PV cell power plant near Leipzig in Germany, comprises 500,000 separate solar cells over an area the size of 200 football pitches. The power the plant produces is about one-tenth of that of an average coal-fired power plant occupying a much smaller area of land. However, the difference between the two lessens when the area of land affected by mining for fuel is included.

▼ Protestors in many countries are concerned about the way wind turbines transform the countryside, such as in the South Downs, UK.

Biomass issues

Biomass is the main form of energy for heating or cooking for one-third of the world's population. Mostly these are people in poorer countries who collect wood and animal dung for fuel. Biomass in power stations and biofuels in vehicles supply only about 3 per cent of the energy used in more economically developed countries, but they are growing in popularity. Supporters of biomass expansion argue that biomass is environmentally sustainable. They say that using biomass, such as crop residues and waste wood or rubbish, disposes of waste that would otherwise cause environmental problems. Supporters of biomass also say that burning biomass crops has a neutral effect on the atmosphere as it is simply returning the carbon dioxide that was taken in by the plants during their growth.

However, their argument does not take into account the large amount of energy used to cultivate, harvest, transport and process biomass into fuels. For example, waste wood and crops, such as straw, need to be chopped into small pieces and dried. They are sometimes formed into tightly packed bricks, or heated to make charcoal, all using machines, before they can burn efficiently. Even then, biomass is a far less concentrated source of carbon than fossil fuels, so it releases less energy.

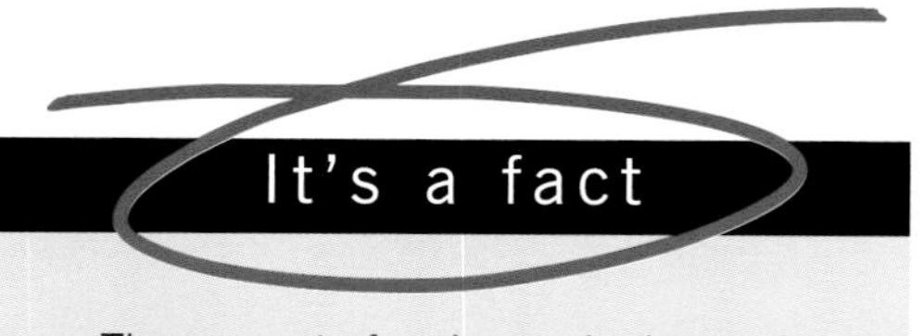

The amount of grain required to make enough biofuel to fill the tank of a 4x4 vehicle once is sufficient to feed one person for a whole year.

viewpoints

'Co-firing with biomass is a reasonable way forward; it's a logical extension of what they're [some power stations] already doing.'

Neil Crumpton, Friends of the Earth

'The benefits of biofuels cannot be achieved at the expenses of increased food shortages, environmental degradation and poverty.'

Celso Marcatto, Food Rights Coordinator, ActionAid, Brazil

Knock-on effects of biofuels

Farmers can make more money growing crops for fuel than they can growing crops for food. Worldwide, much of the land available for farming is already being farmed. If farmers use up more space for biomass fuel, this will mean that more people could go hungry.

If farmers in one country change the crops they are growing, this can have a global impact on the prices of crops and land use in other countries, too. For example, when the United States encouraged its bioethanol industry (see page 4), many US soy bean farmers started to grow maize instead, because they could make more money selling maize for biofuel than they could for soy beans grown for food and cattle feed. This change in crop meant that there was a decrease in global soy bean farming and, as a result, the soy that was available fetched a higher price. Following this, farmers in other countries, such as Brazil, started to grow soy to make more money. They also grew more sugar cane for export to the United States, as this crop produces more bioethanol per kilogram than maize and given the demand for biofuel, it commands a higher price.

▲ Expansion of oil palm plantations, partly grown to make biofuels, is driving deforestation in countries rich in tropical rainforest, such as Indonesia.

In some cases, farming soy and sugar cane had a serious effect on the environment because Brazilian farmers cleared part of the Amazon rainforest to make more crop land. Deforestation not only removes trees that absorb carbon dioxide, but it also produces large emissions of greenhouse gases as farmers burn leftover stumps of trees after timber has been removed to clear land. Removing forest also displaces people and wildlife and exposes soil to erosion.

The pros and cons of hydropower

Hydropower produces the most power of any renewable energy reource worldwide, and about one-sixth of all power. The smallest hydropower schemes divert river water via turbines. The biggest involve damming large rivers, creating reservoirs and controlling the release of water through the dam via turbines. Some schemes, such as the Three Gorges dam in China (see page 30) and Itaipu dam in Brazil, are vast technological triumphs that can bring employment to remote mountainous areas and immense quantities of renewable power. They may also prevent flooding downstream, supply drinking water and offer recreation space.

However, the act of damming and reservoir creation can cause problems, especially the mass displacement of people. Around the world, up to 80 million people have been displaced by about 50,000 dam projects. Dams also slow water flow downstream, which although this may prevent flooding of settlements, it can affect habitats for wildlife and industries including fishing and shipping suffer. Particles of rock and soil, usually washed downstream, may get trapped behind a dam. They can collect in reservoirs and cause them to overflow.

case study

Hydropower for China

The three Gorges dam on the Yangtse river, China is the biggest dam in the world, with a reservoir 660 kilometres long. This single hydropower facility can generate as much electricity as ten nuclear power plants. While supporters of the dam hail its success, critics point out that behind these impressive statistics are growing environmental problems.

Pollution of reservoir water is a growing problem because the dam is preventing the river from washing the pollution downstream. Human sewage from the growing Chinese population is still pouring into the river. Fertilizers and pesticides are washing off farmland into upstream tributaries, feeding into the reservoir. The tributaries are becoming choked with algae because they are thriving on the fertilizer-rich water. Poisonous chemicals are also being released from submerged buildings as they decay underwater. In addition, the rising volume of water is soaking into and putting pressure on the banks of the Yangtse river. Around 40 kilometres of riverbank has already caved in. The weight of water in the reservoir and the heavy dam structures may also be responsible for increased earthquakes in the area, which further cause riverbanks to shake loose. When large amounts of soil and rock hit the water they can create waves. The biggest of these are up to 50 metres high and have killed people working nearby or on Yangtse tributaries.

In response, the Chinese government has closed or moved over 1,000 factories from the banks. It has also spent US$400 million (£200 million) on stabilizing the river banks and building many water treatment plants to clean up the polluted water.

▼ It took 17 years to build the Three Gorges dam in China, the world's largest dam.

▲ All animal life has been killed in this stream as polluted water from a reservoir flows through it.

Emission problems

Supporters of hydropower schemes argue that hydropower generates electricity without emissions. However, critics of the schemes point out that this ignores the evidence about pollution caused by dams and reservoirs.

To make a structure strong enough to hold back a reservoir, engineers use vast quantities of concrete. Itaipu dam in Brazil is made of enough concrete to build over 200 football stadiums. Every tonne of cement made releases 1 tonne of carbon dioxide from machinery and from chemical changes in the concrete mix. Carbon dioxide is not the only gas emitted by hydropower schemes. Methane is released when flooded vegetation rots under the reservoir water and bacteria create methane when feeding on the mix of broken-down plants and sediment in the water at the bottom of reservoirs. Methane traps up to 25 times more heat in the atmosphere than carbon dioxide. Hydropower schemes can emit ten times more greenhouse gases than wind power per unit of electricity generated because of reservoir emissions.

It's a fact

Reservoirs around the world are responsible for over 100 million tonnes of methane, a harmful greenhouse gas.

summary

- Renewable energy produces few emissions directly in creating power but substantial amounts of pollution from dams and turbines.
- Renewable energy can be used at a small scale for microgeneration in isolated settings.
- Some renewables cannot produce a reliable supply of power.

CHAPTER 5

World energy issues

As the global population increases and the standard of living changes, people will be using more and more power. How soon will the world run out of non-renewables? How are people making these resources last to put off that day? And what effects do energy resources have on global relations?

Fast-developing world

A combination of increasing population and changing standards of living is resulting in a growing demand for energy resources. China plans to build 500 coal-fired power plants during the next decade, which will increase emissions. But its development, as in many developing economies, is not totally reliant on polluting power technologies. China is also leading the world in less-polluting renewable power. For example, generation by wind power is doubling each year, especially in the windy regions of western China and Mongolia, and is expected to be generate as much electricity as fossil fuel power plants by 2015. However, for countries struggling to supply their citizens with sufficient clean water or food, choosing cheaper, polluting energy options over more expensive, cleaner ones may be difficult to avoid.

Although China has the largest population of any country in the world, this is increasing at a slower rate than India's population. Between 1995 and 2025, the population of India is expected to grow by over 400 million people. The Indian economy is growing by about 8 per cent per year, partly as a result of thriving global industries such as information technology (IT). This increase in wealth has meant that more

▼ The power demands of expanding industry, such as this factory in China, are putting a growing pressure on world energy resources.

people can afford to own their own cars. In 2008, car ownership in India was three times that of 1998 and it is expected to treble again by 2020. More industry and more transport in India means more fossil fuels are used. However, many people say that it is unfair to blame fast-developing countries for dwindling non-renewables. For example, although by 2020 there could be as many as 100 cars per 1,000 citizens in India, in the United States there are already nearly 500 per 1,000.

case study

A car for the masses

In 2008, India's giant Tata motor corporation developed the Nano. The company plans to sell this tiny car for just 100,000 rupees (about US$2,000 or £1,000). This 5-seater is the world's cheapest production car and is available to many Indians who, up until now, could afford only a scooter. Critics of the cheap car say that it will cause vast emission problems. The Guardian newspaper in the UK said 'India's vehicles spewed 219 million tonnes of carbon dioxide into the atmosphere in 2005. Experts say that figure will jump almost seven-fold to 1,470 million tonnes by 2035 if car travel remains unchecked.' This impact on the environment is undoubtedly a bad thing, but is it double standards for countries such as the United States and the UK to blame less developed countries when the travel addiction of richer countries already damages the atmosphere so much? Do the Indians have the same right to motoring as people in more developed countries?

▲ In 2008, Ratan Tata of the Tata motor corporation presented the Nano at the 78th International Motor Show in Geneva, Switzerland.

When will oil flowing from the world's offshore oilfields slow to a trickle, making rigs relics of the past?

How much oil is left?

There is a big debate over how much oil is left in the world. Oil companies say there are larger reserves than supporters of renewable energy claim are left. Some people fear the oil companies make these claims only to show that they are confident in keeping up with the future demand for oil. For example, in the 1980s, the main oil-producing countries in the Middle East stated that there was a large increase of approximately 300 billion barrels in their reserves even though, during this time, no significant discoveries of new oil were made.

Many scientists believe that twice as much oil is being consumed than is being discovered. Others insist that the world has passed or is fast approaching peak oil, a point when supply has reached maximum output, and therefore will shrink, and demand will further outstrip supply. Between 2001 and 2008, the price

It's a fact

The scientist M. King Hubbert came up with a way of calculating peak oil based on discoveries of oil fields. In 1956, he predicted peak oil production from US oilfields would occur between 1965 and 1970. Most scientists agree that his calculations were accurate. The United States has been importing more oil each year since 1970.

of oil surged from US$30 (£15) to US$147 (£73) per barrel. The higher price is not only the result of a diminishing supply, but also because there are not enough refineries, which are the factories that make petrol and diesel from oil. No new refineries have been built in the United States in 29 years and Europe's last refinery was built in 1989. This is partly because some of today's oil tankers refine as they transport oil around the oceans. Nevertheless, fuel demand has risen greatly and oil companies are struggling to meet consumer demand.

Stretching out what's left

Some economists are more optimistic about the volume of remaining oil resources. They think that as oil becomes more expensive, oil companies will be forced to put more effort into and spend more on finding oil. This is already happening. Existing data suggest that the proportion of oil produced per unit area of world oil fields increased from 22 per cent in 1980 to 35 per cent in 2004. This was possible through improved oil detection technology and more efficient drilling and other extraction technologies.

Assuming the higher cost of extracting oil drops over time, oil prices could decrease and oil may last several decades longer than originally predicted. However, this is not really a viable long-term outlook. In 2005, a BP study into remaining oil supplies stated that nearly all countries are expected to 'run dry' of oil before 2100. Supporters of renewable energy resources ask whether it is shortsighted to put a lot of effort into extracting oil at the expense of developing renewable energy and cutting emissions fast enough to slow climate change.

case study

Speeding up gas formation

New technology may be able to unlock the potential of solid oil, which cannot flow out of wells conventionally, by turning it into gas. Such oil was previously thought to be economically unrecoverable owing to the high costs of technology to bring it to the surface. However, scientists from Newcastle, UK, and Calgary, Canada, universities fed a special nutrient mixture to bacteria that live on oil. The bacteria thrived and multiplied and digested the oil into methane within a few months. In natural conditions, this degradation of oil takes tens of millions of years. The team now plans to pump the nutrients deep down into exhausted oil wells in western Canada. It is hoped that gas will start to flow out of the wells in a few years. The team believes its technique could prolong the life of any oil well by over 20 years.

viewpoints

'We are unquestionably moving from having a world with growing pools of cheap oil to dwindling supplies of expensive oil.'
Johann Hari, The Independent, 29 May 2008

'An imminent peak in production has been repeatedly and wrongly predicted. It's not a resource issue, it's an investment issue.'
Peter Davies, special economic advisor to BP oil company, 2008

The new reserves

Oil companies are finding new reserves each year. Recent finds include the Kashagan field in Kazakhstan, regions in sub-Saharan Africa and also Nyuni island in south-eastern Tanzania. These are all 'conventional' finds of liquid oil trapped in rock.

Known reserves of 'unconventional' oil are much greater. They include large areas of tar sands that have been found in Canada and Venezuela. Tar sand is sand into which deeper oil reserves of the past have soaked. Unconventional oil also includes oil shale, found in countries such as Canada and Germany. Oil shale is a soft rock containing carbon that is not quite oil. Both tar sand and oil shale need to be mined and heated to extract the oil. This consumes a lot of energy and creates emissions. For example, oil shale production creates more than four times as much greenhouse gas as conventional oil production. It uses around 40 per cent of the energy the shale oil can release, and consumes and pollutes vast quantities of water. Experts have worked out that the cost of developing existing reserves and exploring new ones between 2008 and 2013 could be nearly US$2 trillion (£1 trillion). Critics of schemes to develop existing reserves question whether this money could be better used to further develop renewables. For example, that sum would pay for over 3,000 large offshore wind farms each with 60 turbines.

Tackling emissions

Coal supply is considered fairly secure – it should last for around 160 years at current rates of use. It is thought that coal

▼ This refinery in Kazakhstan has been built to accomodate the newly found oil fields in the region.

Tar sands are part of the world's unconventional oil reserves.

will remain central to power generation globally during this time, so many countries are finding ways to tackle the coal emission problem rather than reduce coal use. The biggest hope for the future is burying the problem. Carbon capture and storage (CCS) is when the carbon dioxide from power stations is captured and pumped into underground spaces. Spaces that could be used for CCS are the gaps left after oil or gas has been extracted from reserves. The carbon dioxide can even help to force more oil out of the rock, increasing recovery of oil from reserves. A scheme proposed for the Miller oil and gas reserve, Scotland, UK, will convert the methane in gas into hydrogen, which may be burnt in special power stations with zero emissions, and carbon dioxide for CCS. The trouble is that CCS technology is not yet proven. It is likely to be very expensive and use a lot of energy to capture, compress and pipe the gas underground. Even then, what if the carbon dioxide simply leaks out into the atmosphere through cracks in the rocks?

'Co-firing'

At present, some power stations are tackling emissions by co-firing, or burning a small percentage of biomass with coal in power stations. Biomass emits less carbon dioxide than coal and when mixed with coal produces a similar amount of heat, so power stations can generate just as efficiently. Europe's biggest coal-fired power station, Drax in Yorkshire, UK, aims to save 2 million tonnes of carbon dioxide each year by co-firing. Some people question whether Drax owners really are caring for the atmosphere by co-firing. After all, total annual Drax carbon dioxide emissions are still more than the total from all cars in the UK. Or is it the case that some contribution to emission cuts is better than none?

Trading carbon

The Kyoto Protocol emission reduction targets are proving difficult to meet for some countries and the industries within them. Initial emission targets are based on the number of people in a country and the level of industrial development. The targets vary by country. On average, countries worldwide have agreed to cut their 1990 emission levels by 5 per cent by 2012. However, some richer countries with lots of industry, such as the UK, need to reduce much more than this, while other, poorer countries with little industry and fewer cars on the roads can actually emit more and still stay within their targets. The drive to reduce emissions has established a global carbon trade. This relies on the principle of offsetting where one country, one region or one power company can buy carbon credits off another.

For example, if the UK is emitting 1 million tonnes of carbon dioxide more than its target amount and India 1 million tonnes less, the UK could then buy carbon credits from India worth 1 million tonnes. The credit money would pay for new low-emission projects such as wind farms or hydropower schemes in India. It could also pay for emission absorbers such as tree plantations, or systems to capture methane produced by livestock. Individuals may also offset, for example by paying to plant trees after going on a holiday abroad.

◀ Thousands of New Yorkers walk along the Brooklyn Bridge away from Manhattan on 14 August 2003. New York City along with major cities along the northeast corridor, experienced a major power cut, causing disruptions to transport and communication.

In 1973, the major oil-producing countries of the Middle East raised the price of oil and stopped exporting it to the United States and other countries. The move was a response to the United States supporting Israel in its Yom Kippur war against Egypt and Syria. The effect was fuel rationing and many affected businesses as the United States ran out of oil stocks.

Companies work out how many trees would be needed to absorb the carbon dioxide produced by the aeroplane getting to and from the destination.

Offsetting is hotly debated. Many people say that it is not ethical for a highly polluting nation to use its wealth to buy emissions from elsewhere. They also say that it lets governments, industries and individuals off the hook from facing the consequences of polluting behaviour and does not encourage bold emission-saving measures. Supporters of carbon trading say that by giving a value to emissions it provides a financial incentive to cut emissions. They say that it should encourage renewable, low-emission projects.

Security issues

Another major issue in world energy is security. Power and fuel supply is so integral to people's lives that when the supply is suddenly cut off, it can cause disarray. Power outages (power cuts) are not unusual in less developed countries such a Nepal, but people in more developed countries are used to an uninterrupted supply of power.

In August 2003, an accidental power outage in northeastern North America, including the cities of New York, Toronto and Detroit, affected around 50 million people. The power vital for transport, communication, water supply, industry and other aspects of life disappeared. This outage was short-lived but it reminded people of the importance of security at large power stations. Power stations are obvious targets for any terrorists intent on disrupting life in a city, region or country.

There are other security issues concerning energy resources. When the major world supplies of fossil fuels are in the Middle East and Russia, other countries relying on these resources are vulnerable. Around 70 per cent of global oil and gas is consumed by North America, Europe and East Asia, but these regions hold only around 12 per cent of conventional reserves. If political circumstances make supply difficult, the countries might grind to a halt. Fuel security is an issue that can cause conflict. Some people argue that the US invasion of Iraq in 2003 was to do with keeping access to Iraq's oil reserves rather than the stated aim of fighting terrorism and preserving human rights for Iraqis.

summary

- Emissions are soaring in developing nations as they industrialize and standards of living improve.
- The amount of oil left on Earth is an issue of debate, but coal supplies will last longer.
- Emission-cutting targets have led to emission trading between high and low emitters.
- Energy security is an important world issue.

CHAPTER 6

Energy futures

▲ Power is created from waste – a pipe carries methane from a landfill site for use as fuel.

The energy resources debate is not just about how people can get the energy they need to power their lives without damaging the Earth. It is also about how people across the globe can better use energy to place less demand on the resources we have.

Take energy efficiency seriously

The International Energy Agency (IEA) predicts that global energy use is set to increase by 50–60 per cent by 2030. If this demand is met by fossil fuels, the greenhouse effect could be 50 per cent higher than it is today. The drive towards renewable energy sources is very important in cutting emissions, yet may have less effect on the atmosphere than simply preventing energy waste. Energy efficiency is a bit like making each unit of energy work harder. Many countries worldwide have long promoted energy efficiency because it saves money. For example, power consumption in the United States is about half what it was in 1970, as measured per dollar of economic output, simply because more energy-efficient machines work using less power. However, in the twenty-first century, the biggest reason to be efficient is to reduce emissions.

There is a wide variety of ways in which individuals can save energy by changing behaviour, such as turning down the central heating and switching off electrical appliances rather than leaving them on standby. They can buy energy-saving appliances from light bulbs to fridges. Scientists have calculated that if the Chinese government insisted on using the best energy-saving technology in all the air conditioners and refrigerators in China, then by 2030 it would be saving twice the amount of energy each year as the Three Gorges hydropower plant generates (see page 30). Many industries can become more energy-efficient. For example, most fossil fuel-fired power stations release heat while generating and this is usually wasted when hot water from steam cools. In the UK, power stations waste about 60 per cent of the heat energy they produce enough to heat every house in the country. Many people say that this is wrong and that governments should insist that power stations capture heat and put it to good use. The combined heat and power plant in Vaxjo, Sweden, has reduced the town's carbon dioxide emissions by 69 per cent over seven years.

Conservation and development

Some people argue that using less energy can limit development. Poorer people do not always have access to efficient, energy-saving machines. What right do richer countries have to say that poorer countries should be energy efficient during industrial expansion, when they were not during their own development? In addition, some people question whether energy efficiency really does reduce energy use and emissions. They use analogies such as passenger aeroplanes. When wide-bodied passenger aircraft were introduced in the 1960s to replace smaller aeroplanes, people predicted there would be fewer flights. However, each passenger paid less as more could fit on the bigger aeroplanes. This led to greater demand for air travel, more airraft, more fuel used and greater emissions. By that logic, energy-efficient appliances might simply make people feel happier about using them more!

▼ Some individuals install solar cells on their roofs to generate their own power and reduce their contribution to greenhouse emissions.

Fuel efficiency

Governments have long tried to get people to travel without cars not only to cut emissions, but also to ease road congestion. This is a major problem in cities, causing increased atmospheric pollution. Strategies include establishing bike lanes, mass public transport systems such as underground railways, and congestion charges. However, the biggest energy-efficiency successes have been in car technology and design. In the 1970s, an average US car could travel about 5.5 kilometres on a litre of fuel. Then the price of oil rose, so car makers developed more fuel-efficient engines, more aerodynamic designs and used lighter materials to make smaller cars that used less fuel. By the 1980s average fuel efficiency was 10.5 km per litre. Today, the most economical cars use less than one-third of fuel than this. Some are hybrid cars with special engines that run on petrol or diesel when going fast, but switch to a battery-operated electric motor when driving slowly.

It's a fact

The United States produces nearly 10 million tonnes of hydrogen each year. This would be enough fuel to run 30 million cars, but there are only a few hundred hydrogen cars in the country. Most liquid hydrogen is used to power space rockets or shuttles, and in industrial processes.

Even with energy-saving car technology, people rarely drive in the most economical ways. For example, people can improve fuel efficiency by 3 per cent by pumping up their tyres fully and 10 per cent by changing the car engine's air filter regularly. Driving behaviour also makes a difference. For example, accelerating fast and braking hard

▼ Urban transport of the future? This bus is fuelled with hydrogen and emits only steam as it drives along in Rejkyavik, Iceland.

uses more fuel than driving slowly and steadily. What is more, richer people are often still buying bigger, 'performance' cars by choice. The only proven way to wean people off this bad car habit is to make them pay higher taxes for driving gas-guzzling cars.

Future fuel?

All of the major car manufacturers are developing cars that run on hydrogen, with the hope that it is the fuel of the future. The advantage of hydrogen as a fuel is that it does not pollute when it releases energy. Cars with special fuel cells can use hydrogen fuel to make electricity to power an electric motor. One problem with hydrogen is that it needs a lot of energy to make it and at present the commonest way to produce hydrogen is using fossil fuel power, mostly by processing gas, which creates carbon dioxide emissions. In future, solar power systems may be able to split water to release hydrogen. Another problem is storage of the gas. Hydrogen takes up a lot of space so it is only economical to store it as a liquid. This can be achieved only if hydrogen is kept very cold and under pressure, and this requires heavy, reinforced tanks that add a lot of weight to cars.

Many people think that it is better to concentrate on creating power renewably to charge batteries that run cars. They say that using electricity to generate hydrogen, and more energy to transport and store it, before running hydrogen through a cell to make electricity does not make sense! With improved batteries, electric cars of the future should be able to run further between charges than electric cars of the past.

viewpoints

'We do have a national energy policy – it's basically to keep wasting lots of energy; import it at whatever price, by whatever means necessary; keep stealing from our kids and keep screwing up the climate.'
Amory Lovins, Chief Scientist, Rocky Mountain Institute

'Energy efficiency gains can increase energy consumption by two means: by making energy appear effectively cheaper... and by increasing economic growth, which pulls up energy use.'
Harry Saunders, Does Energy Conservation Worsen Global Warming?, 1992

case study

A green way to drive trains

Freightmiser is an Australian invention to help train drivers cut fuel use. It is a computer-based system with a screen in the cab of the train that displays changing information about the route as the train moves along. The system automatically calculates the optimal speed and fuel use in order to travel the route to schedule, but also using the least fuel possible. It advises drivers exactly when to brake to make the most efficient use of slopes to speed up or slow down the train. When drivers follow Freightmiser's guidance they can save between 8 and 16 per cent of fuel. This saves a lot of money and cuts emissions. In 2008, the Freightmiser was trialled on Indian trains. Indian Railways transports 16 million passengers and 1 million tonnes of freight each day. The diesel or power bill for running the trains is US$2 billion (£1 billion) each year. Using Freightmiser, Indian Railways could save millions.

▲ Pelamis generates power faster as the ocean waves get stronger.

New water power

It is likely that the next generation of water power will not be from large reservoir hydropower but from different sources. New technologies that use wave power include Pelamis, a hinged row of floats that are the length of a football pitch, and the Limpet. When a wave moves past Pelamis, each float in turn rises and falls and this motion forces oil through tubes past a mini-turbine that turns a generator. The first Pelamis wave farm is already operating off the Portugese coast. In the Limpet, which is built onto coastal rocks, rising waves force air one way, and falling waves then force it the other way past a turbine. Experimental buoys have already been developed. These generate power when special plastic streamers flex in the water. Water power may also enter the home. Scientists are developing cheap mini-turbines that fit inside domestic water pipes and systems that generate electricity when people turn on a tap.

case study

Desert power for Europe

In November 2007, Prince Hassan of Jordan presented an idea to the European Parliament for a vast network of solar power plants near the North African coast skirting the Sahara. His idea was to capture the abundant solar power of the desert and transport it to Europe. The Desertec organization, supported by Prince Hassan, plans to use mirror arrays that track the Sun's movement across the sky to heat a central receiver which, in turn, heats water to make steam for generation. Heat will be stored overnight using tanks of molten salt. Some of the heat may be used to convert seawater into fresh water, a scarce resource in the Middle East. The electricity will be imported using a new network of high-voltage cables under the Mediterranean Sea, which lose less power during transmission than present power grids. Such a vast scheme will cost over US$400 billion (£200 billion) and therefore needs to be financed by many countries, especially the richer European countries. Germany and Algeria are already laying cables between their two countries, and a pilot plant is almost operational in Egypt. If all goes to plan, then in 30 years the Desertec network could be generating one-sixth of Europe's power at the same cost as hydropower today.

Next step for solar

Solar power expansion has been held back for years by expensive technology, but there are now cheaper solar cells in development that could drive a solar revolution. Nanosolar has produced a new type of solar cell that is printed similarly to a newspaper onto aluminium foil, and therefore is flexible and light. This process will potentially halve the price of making solar cell panels that are also more portable and adaptable than those used in the past. Cells could be printed onto a wide range of surfaces, from car roofs to windows. Scientists are also trying to work around one limitation of solar power, which is the need to store power in batteries. To do this, Japanese scientists have invented solar photocapacitors in flexible, plastic sheets that store the power they generate.

summary

- One way to meet future energy needs is to be energy efficient for example by driving, using less fuel or capturing waste heat from power stations.
- Transport fuel of the future may be hydrogen if it can be produced without power generated from fossil fuels.
- Ocean and solar power are likely to be major players in the future renewables mix.

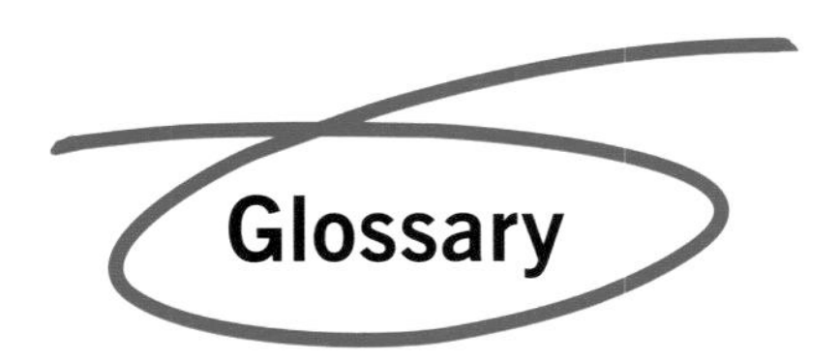

Glossary

Acid rain Rainwater containing dissolved gases that can cause environmental damage.

Carbon capture and storage (CCS) A method of removing carbon dioxide from gases released by fossil fuels in power stations, and storing it in underground rocks.

Carbon credit A way of giving carbon emissions a value that can be traded.

Carbon trading The process of buying and selling carbon credits.

Co-firing Burning biomass with non-renewable fuel.

Dam A structure or barrier that contains or blocks the flow of water.

Emission The release of substances, such as gases, into the environment.

Fuel efficiency A measure of how much work a machine does, such as distance travelled, with a given volume of fuel.

kinetic energy Movement energy.

Kyoto Protocol An agreement made between 137 countries in Kyoto, Japan, in 1997 to reduce greenhouse gas emissions to below 1990 levels by 2012.

Microgeneration The small-scale generation of electricity from renewable resources by communities, small businesses and individuals to meet their own power needs.

Off-grid Not connected to power lines and without access to electricity made in large power stations.

Offsetting A method of balancing or cancelling out the amount of greenhouse gases produced in an activity through investments made in projects that reduce emissions, such as planting new trees.

Oil refinery Factories that make petrol and diesel from oil.

Particulate pollution Pollution of the atmosphere by tiny particles of soot mostly released in exhaust gases from engines burning fossil fuels.

Photosynthesis The production of food by green plants from water and carbon dioxide using sunlight.

Photovoltaic (PV) cell A device made from stacked, thin layers of material, such as silicon, which produces electricity when exposed to sunlight.

Radioactive waste Waste comprising spent nuclear fuel, tools and clothing used by workers in nuclear power plants, that releases gamma radiation.

Renewable energy resources Resources such as wood, sunlight and waves that can be replaced or which never run out following conversion into energy.

Solar array A group of connected panels of solar cells that together generate electricity.

Unconventional oil Oil not found in discrete liquid reserves within spaces in rocks. Tar sand and oil shale are the most common types of unconventional oil.

Timeline

1830–1839 Michael Faraday builds a dynamo to change kinetic energy into electrical energy.

1839 The first fuel cell is developed by Sir William Robert Grove.

1855 Benjamin Stillman discovers that crude oil can be refined into kerosene.

1859 Colonel Edwin Drake first drills for oil in the United States in Titusville, Pensylvannia.

1876 Nicolaus Otto builds the first internal combustion engine that runs on ethanol.

1880 Auguste Mouchot demonstrates a solar-powered printing press.

1883 Charles Fritts creates a solar cell.

1890 Mass production of automobiles (cars) begins, creating demand for gasoline (petrol).

1895–1896 Niagara Falls hydropower station opens on the United States/Canada border.

1904 A geothermal power plant opens in Italy.

1908 The first major oil strike occurs in the Middle East.

1954 The world's first nuclear power plant starts generating electricity in Russia.

1951 Saudi Arabia puts the world's largest oil field into production.

1958 PV cells are used to power the US space satellite *Vanguard*.

1973 An OPEC oil embargo causes oil prices in United States to rise four-fold.

1977 The Trans-Alaska pipeline is completed.

1986 The Chernobyl nuclear reactor accident.

1993 The United States imports more oil and other refined products than it produces.

1997 Kyoto Protocol sets out greenhouse gas reductions required of the countries who sign.

2008 The price of oil rises to the highest price ever (US$147 per barrel).

Further information

Books:

Energy Crisis (World Issues)
Ewan McLeish (Franklin Watts, 2007)

Coal, Oil and Gas (Energy Debate)
Sally Morgan (Wayland, 2007)

Geothermals and Bio-energy (Looking at Energy) Fiona Reynoldson (Wayland, 2005)

Websites:

www.suntrek.org/earth-beyond/earths-energy-resources/earths-energy-resources.shtml
A website with clear information about different energy resources.

www.foe.co.uk/campaigns/climate/issues/climate_change_index.html
Log on to find out more about Friends of the Earth's campaign against climate change.

www.guardian.co.uk/environment/energy
This is an excellent source of current news stories on energy issues from around the world.

Index

Numbers in **bold** refer to illustrations.

Ethical Debates

Contents of new titles in the series:

Animal Research and Testing
978 0 7502 4818 1

1. Real-life case study
2. What is animal research and testing?
3. The history of animal testing
4. Animal testing in medical research
5. Toxicity tests
6. The use of animals in education
7. Controls, rights and welfare
8. The future of animal research and testing

Birth Control
978 0 7502 5657 5

1. Real-life case study
2. What is birth control?
3. Types of birth control in use today
4. Right or wrong?
5. A human right
6. Health and welfare
7. Population and birth control
8. The role of sex education

Cosmetic Surgery
978 0 7502 5654 4

1. Real-life case study
2. Cosmetic surgery – the basics
3. Is cosmetic surgery harmful?
4. Why try to change your appearance?
5. Looking good, feeling good?
6. Selling cosmetic surgery
7. The business of beauty
8. Society and cosmetic surgery

Energy Resources
978 0 7502 5658 2

1. Real-life case study
2. What are energy resources?
3. Fuels from the past
4. The nuclear option
5. Renewable energy
6. World energy issues
7. Energy futures

Euthanasia
978 0 7502 5655 1

1. Real-life case study
2. What is euthanasia?
3. The doctor's dilemma
4. Choice and control
5. Pushing back the barriers
6. Disabled or dead?
7. Dying with dignity
8. Society and euthanasia today

Tourism
978 0 7502 5656 8

1. Real-life case study
2. What is tourism?
3. Tourism and economics
4. Tourism and local communities
5. Tourism and the environment
6. Sustainable tourism
7. Tourism: good or bad?

WAYLAND